SAMMY'S BIG BOOK OF AWESOME ADVENTURES

SAMMY'S BIG BOOK OF AWESOME ADVENTURES

Illustrated by

Daniel J. Hochstatter

OLIVER NELSON

THOMAS NELSON PUBLISHERS
Nashville • Atlanta • London • Vancouver

Published in Nashville, Tennessee, by Thomas Nelson, Inc., Publishers, and distributed in Canada by Word Communications, Ltd., Richmond, British Columbia.

The Bible version used in this publication is THE NEW KING JAMES VERSION. Copyright ©1979, 1980, 1982, Thomas Nelson, Inc., Publishers.

Printed in the United States of America.

Library of Congress Cataloging-in-Publication Data

ISBN 0-7852-8030-8

1 2 3 4 5 6 — 99 98 97 96 95

SAMMY'S
BIG BOOK
of
Awesome Adventures

It all started because . . .

I am a simple shepherd boy. I spend many hours out in the fields taking care of my sheep. I enjoy being a shepherd, but sometimes I am lonely.

Sammy, one of the younger lambs, seems to know that I am lonely, so he stays close by me. I often tell him stories to make the hours go by more quickly.

My favorite stories are about the people and places in the Bible. I enjoy telling Sammy about Bible heroes and the exciting things that happened to them. He likes to hear about Noah and the ark, David and Goliath, and Joshua and the battle of Jericho. And there are great stories about the life of Jesus and His followers. It's fun to think about what Bible places looked like. I tell Sammy about places like the Red Sea and the Temple in Jerusalem.

The Bible is full of exciting stories, so I never run out of things to talk about. Sammy listens closely and even seems to be imagining what it would be like to be right in the middle of every story.

Look closely at each picture in this book and you will find Sammy and me. Then see if you can find the things listed at the bottom of each page. If you are ready for a really big challenge, try to find the things listed on the pages in the back of the book.

Find Sammy, the Shepherd, and as many of these things as you can.

 Jumping Fish

 Fish Flip

 Monkey Jockey

 Piggy Mud Bath

IN THE GARDEN

—Genesis 1-3

God created a beautiful garden named Eden. He put Adam and Eve in the garden. They were to take care of the plants and animals and enjoy God's company. God gave Adam and Eve everything they needed. But He told them that if they ate the fruit of a certain tree, they would die.

Satan, who was very clever, tricked Eve into eating from that tree. Eve got Adam to eat from it, too.

God made Adam and Eve leave His beautiful garden.

Underwater Headstand

Fast Turtle

Find Sammy, the Shepherd, and as many of these things as you can.

 White Dove

 Party Sheep

 Sheep Angel

 Party Angel

THE SHEPHERDS SEE ANGELS

—Luke 2:8-16

Some shepherds were watching over their sheep in a field outside Bethlehem. It was a quiet, peaceful night, and they were relaxing after a busy day.

Suddenly the peace was shattered by an angel who appeared in the sky. "Do not be afraid," the angel said. "For there is born to you this day in the city of David a Savior, who is Christ the Lord. . . . You will find a Babe wrapped in swaddling cloths, lying in a manger." Then a whole choir of angels appeared and sang, "Glory to God in the highest, and on earth peace, goodwill toward men!"

After the angels left, the shepherds hurried into Bethlehem to see this wonderful new baby!

Bald Angel

Pizza Angel

Find Sammy, the Shepherd, and as many of these things as you can.

 Spaceman

 Unicycle Mouse

 Fisherman

 Twin Babies

COURAGEOUS CODY
VISITS THE CIRCUS

Have you ever had to do something that was really scary? Maybe you had to speak in front of a group of people. Maybe you moved and had to go to a new school.

When you have to try something new, you need courage. *Courage* means being brave enough to try something that scares you.

The circus is full of courageous people. Courageous Cody is one of them. Can you find him?

Parting the Red Seats

Eating on the Job

Courageous Cody

Find Sammy, the Shepherd, and as many of these things as you can.

 Hang In There

 Iguana Pie

 Batty Bat

 Leapfrog

MOUNT ARARAT

God was tired of all the bad things people were doing. No one listened to Him anymore. No one tried to please Him. That is, no one except Noah.

So God told Noah to build a big boat, called an ark. God brought two of every kind of animal on earth and made them go into the ark. Then Noah and his wife and his sons and their wives went into the ark too. God closed the door of the ark.

Soon it started raining outside. It rained for forty days and forty nights. The whole earth was covered with a big flood, but Noah and his family and all the animals were safe because the ark floated on top of the water. Finally the rain ended and the flood waters started to go down. Noah's ark came to rest on the top of Mount Ararat. Noah and his family came out of the ark. They were the only people left on the earth because they loved God.

Hang Time

Frozen Treat Friends

Find Sammy, the Shepherd, and as many of these things as you can.

 Confused Snake

 Upset Fish

 Yanked Fox

 Diver

NOAH'S ARK

—*Genesis 6-7*

People on earth sinned more and more. God saw what was happening and was sorry He had ever created them. God decided to destroy everyone except Noah and his family. They were the only ones who pleased Him.

God told Noah to build a huge boat for himself, his family, and every kind of animal. Building the boat took 120 years, but Noah obeyed God.

When the boat was finished God made it rain forty days and nights. The world was so completely flooded that only Noah, his family, and the animals on the ark survived.

Squirrel Throwing Nuts

Banana Bunch Falling

Find Sammy, the Shepherd, and as many of these things as you can.

 Rope Walker

 Backward Rider

 Balloon Man

 Taxi

THE MISSING BOY

—Luke 2:41-51

Mary and Joseph went to Jerusalem every year to celebrate the Feast of the Passover. When Jesus was twelve years old, He went along.

When the feast was over, everyone began the trip home. Mary and Joseph were walking along with many other people. Jesus wasn't with His parents, but they thought He was probably walking with His cousins or friends. After a whole day of walking they still hadn't seen Jesus, and so they asked a few people about Him. No one had seen Him.

Mary and Joseph went back to Jerusalem. They looked for three days and finally found Jesus in the temple. He was talking with the teachers and asking them questions. Everyone was surprised at how much He understood. Then Jesus went home with His parents because He always obeyed them.

Catch This

Pet Piggy

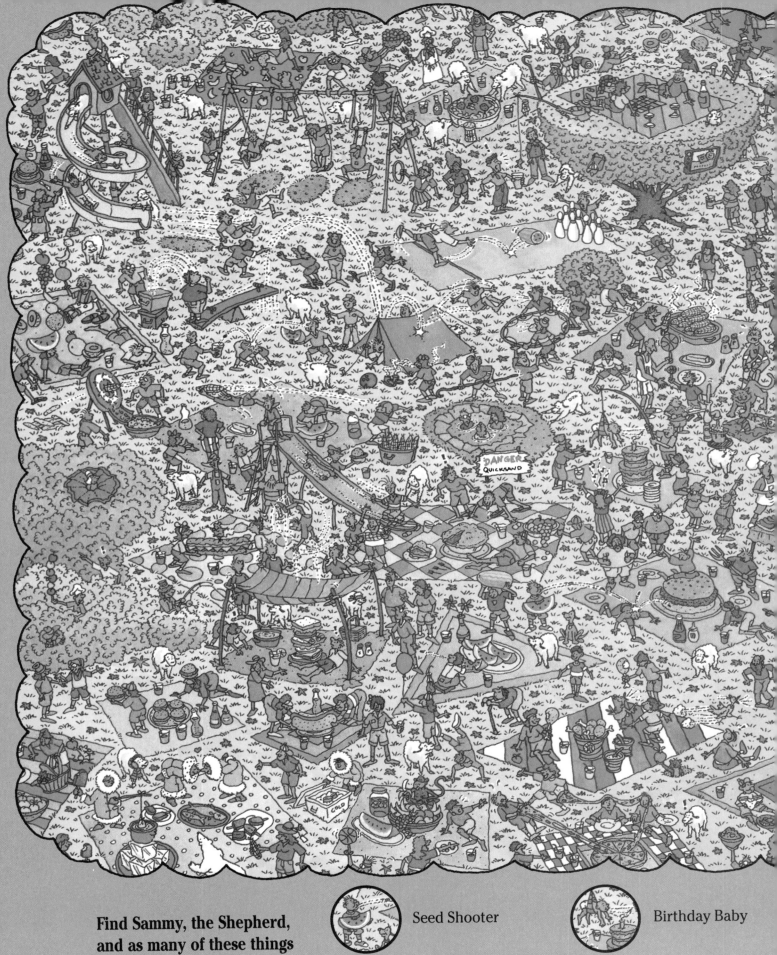

Find Sammy, the Shepherd, and as many of these things as you can.

 Seed Shooter

 Birthday Baby

 Wrong Dog

 What's Cooking?

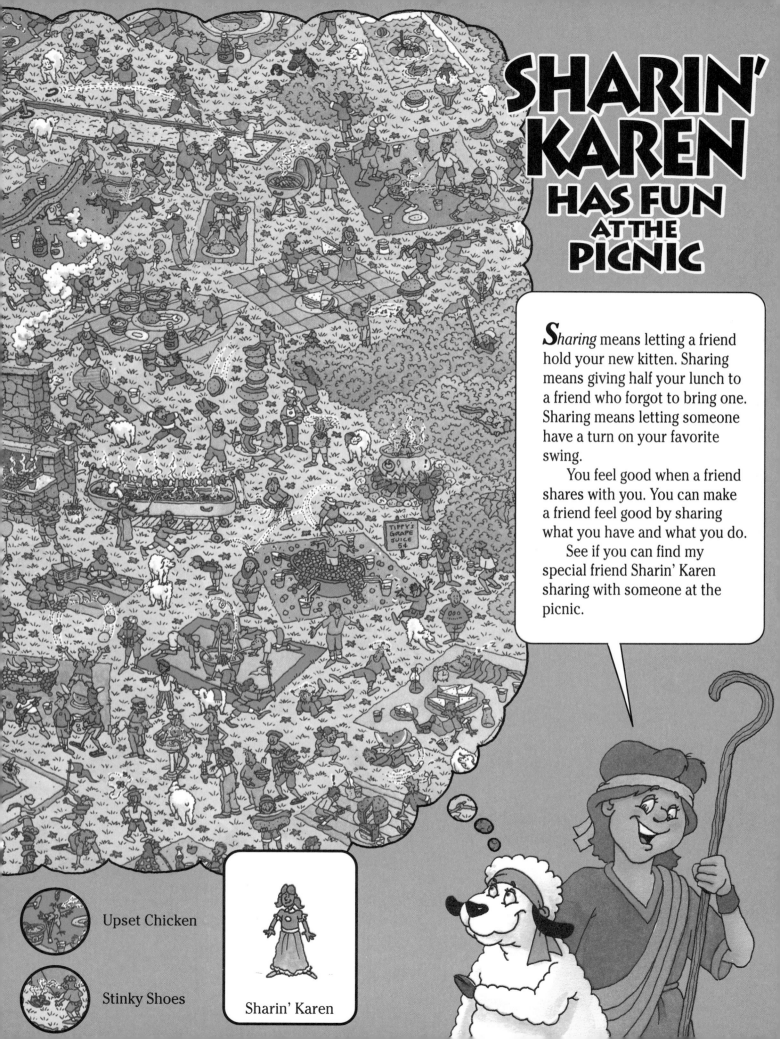

SHARIN' KAREN HAS FUN AT THE PICNIC

Sharing means letting a friend hold your new kitten. Sharing means giving half your lunch to a friend who forgot to bring one. Sharing means letting someone have a turn on your favorite swing.

You feel good when a friend shares with you. You can make a friend feel good by sharing what you have and what you do.

See if you can find my special friend Sharin' Karen sharing with someone at the picnic.

Upset Chicken

Stinky Shoes

Sharin' Karen

Find Sammy, the Shepherd, and as many of these things as you can.

 Book Break

 Leaving Town

 Pitcher of Mouse

 Sherlock Sheep

EGYPT

Jacob was Abraham's grandson. After Jacob became an adult, God gave him the name Israel.

When Israel was very old, there was a famine in the land where he lived. So he and his sons took their families to live in Egypt. Israel's son Joseph already lived there, and he had made sure that everyone in Egypt had plenty of food. As the years passed, the Israelites grew to be a large part of Egypt's population.

Then a new king came to power in Egypt. He did not know about Joseph and the good things he had done for the country. He was afraid of the Israelites because there were so many of them. He thought they might help his enemies if a war broke out. So he made them become slaves of the Egyptians. The Israelites had to work very hard. One of their jobs was to make all the bricks used for the buildings and walls in Egypt. They even built two whole cities for the king.

Cellular Slave

Thirsty Slave

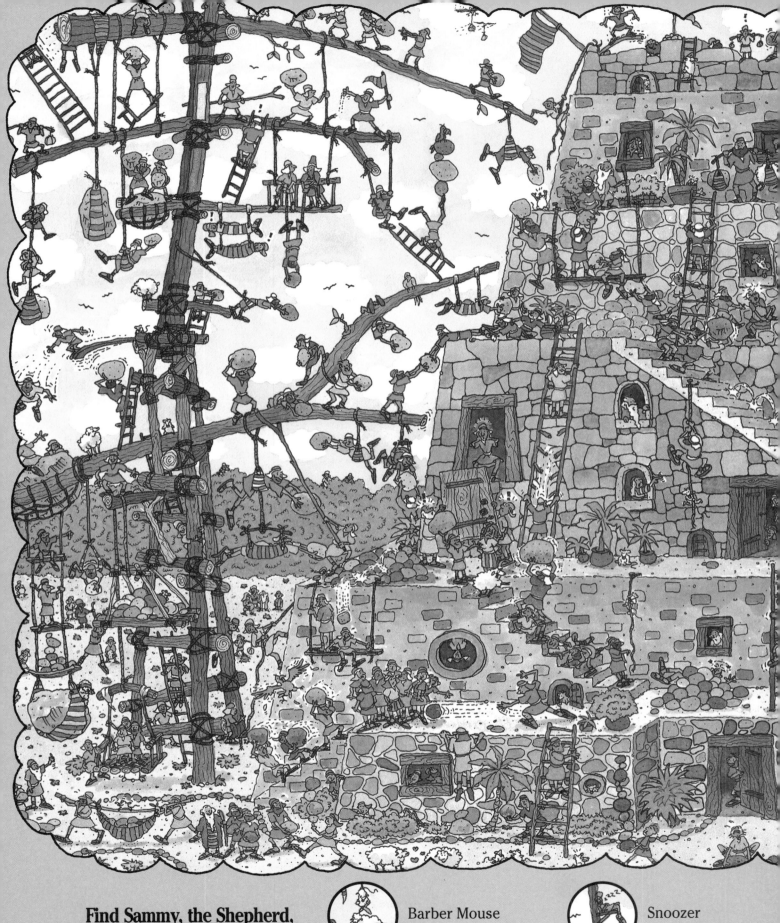

Find Sammy, the Shepherd, and as many of these things as you can.

 Barber Mouse

 Black Sheep

 Snoozer

 Smiling Rock

THE TOWER OF BABEL

—Genesis 11

Long ago everyone on earth spoke the same language. Many of the people lived together on a plain. They decided to build a city with a tower so tall it would reach to the sky. The people wanted to make a name for themselves. But God did not like what they were trying to do with the tower. He made everyone speak a different language.

The city became known as Babel, which means "confusion," because the people could not understand one another.

Mouse in Midair

Mouse on Scaffold

Find Sammy, the Shepherd, and as many of these things as you can.

 Dancing Sheep

 Fish Flipping

 Jumbo Hot Dog

 Boy with Sunglasses

THE FIRST MIRACLE

—John 2:1-11

Jesus and His disciples were invited to a wedding in Cana, a small village in Galilee. Jesus' mother was there too. During the celebration the host ran out of wine to serve the guests. Jesus' mother knew that He could help, so she told the servants to do whatever Jesus asked.

Jesus told the servants to fill six big jars with water. Then He told them to pour some of the water out of the jars. When they did so, they discovered that Jesus had turned the water into wine. This was the first time Jesus did a miracle, and it showed who He was.

Man on Stilts

Tightrope Mouse

Find Sammy, the Shepherd, and as many of these things as you can.

 Got the Point

 Totally Cool

 Fast Food

 Sheepdog

RUTH THE TRUTH
RIDES THE WATERSLIDE

Have you ever known people you could not trust? They might tell you something, but you would not know whether or not it was true.

Being around someone who tells lies is not pleasant. Lies can hurt other people and make them sad. It is best to tell the *truth* always with kindness.

Ruth the Truth always tells the truth, but she does not hurt her friends' feelings. She is gentle with the truth. Can you find her at the water park?

Robin's Good!

Touch–Up–Side Down

Ruth the Truth

Find Sammy, the Shepherd, and as many of these things as you can.

 Rocket Sheep

 Beard Bridge

 Fishy Food Chain

 In a Pinch

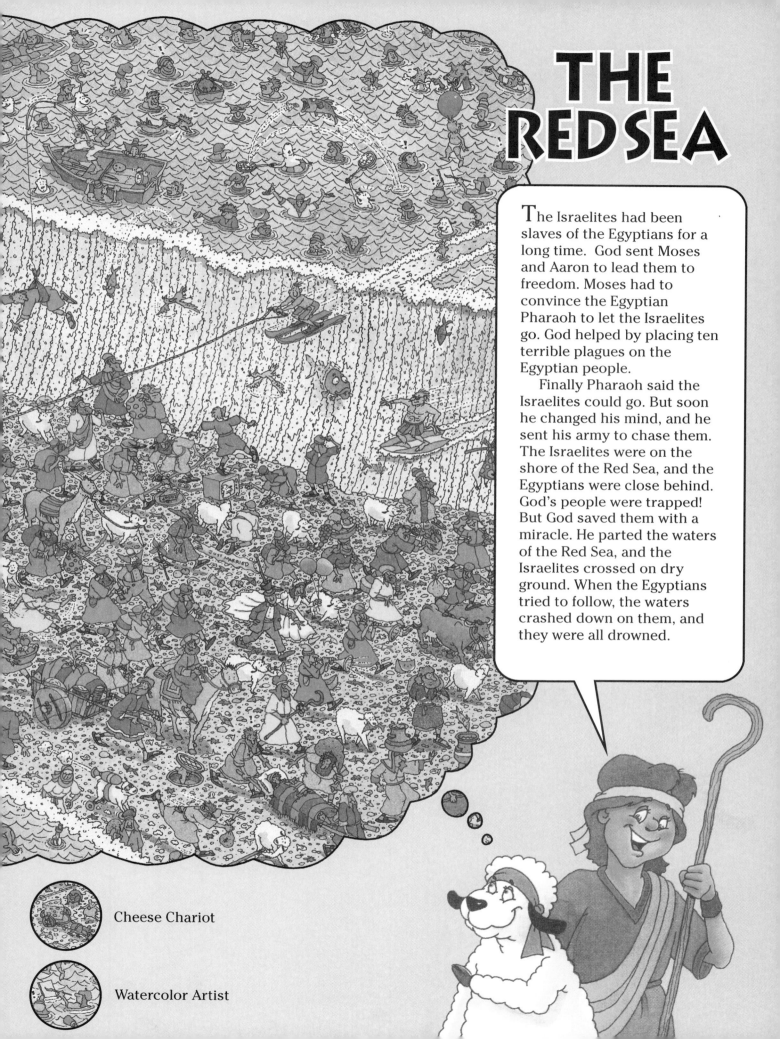

THE RED SEA

The Israelites had been slaves of the Egyptians for a long time. God sent Moses and Aaron to lead them to freedom. Moses had to convince the Egyptian Pharaoh to let the Israelites go. God helped by placing ten terrible plagues on the Egyptian people.

Finally Pharaoh said the Israelites could go. But soon he changed his mind, and he sent his army to chase them. The Israelites were on the shore of the Red Sea, and the Egyptians were close behind. God's people were trapped! But God saved them with a miracle. He parted the waters of the Red Sea, and the Israelites crossed on dry ground. When the Egyptians tried to follow, the waters crashed down on them, and they were all drowned.

Cheese Chariot

Watercolor Artist

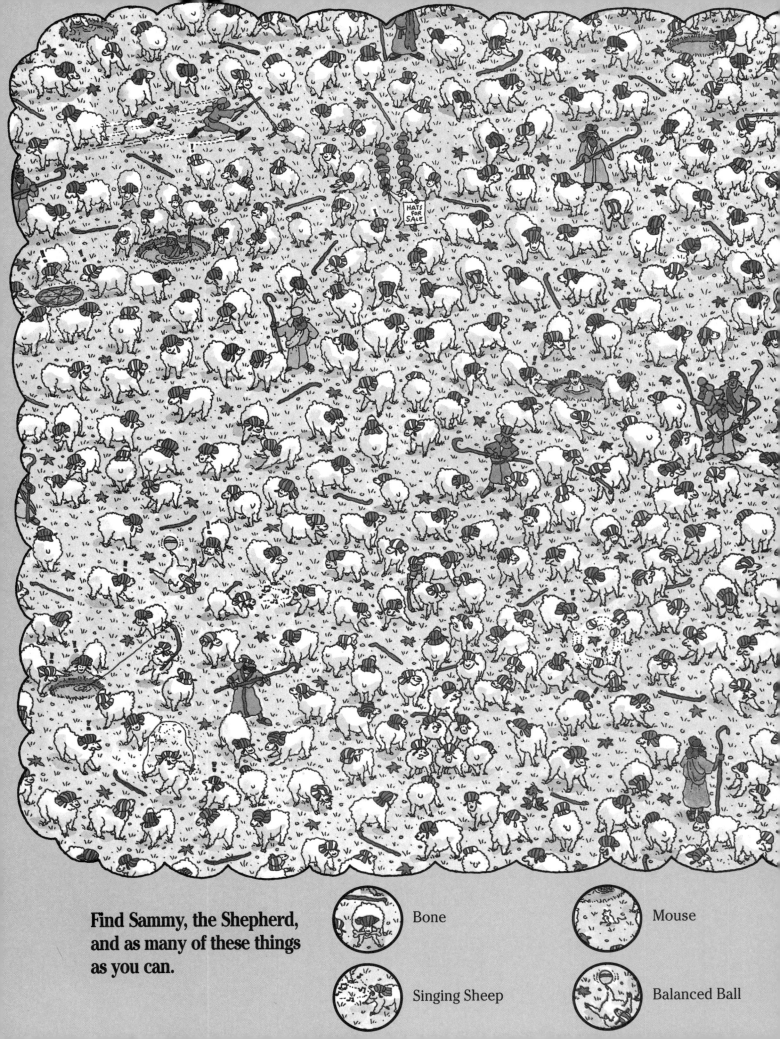

Find Sammy, the Shepherd, and as many of these things as you can.

Bone

Mouse

Singing Sheep

Balanced Ball

THE COLORFUL COAT

—*Genesis 37*

Jacob had twelve sons, but he loved Joseph more than the others. Jacob even made a special coat of many colors for Joseph. That made the brothers very angry, and they would not speak nicely to Joseph.

Joseph had a dream that his brothers would one day bow down to him. When he told them about it, they became even more angry with him. They decided to get rid of him.

Pizza

Black Sheep

Find Sammy, the Shepherd, and as many of these things as you can.

 Drumstick

 Whistler

 Pizza Man

 Woman with Bird

Find Sammy, the Shepherd, and as many of these things as you can.

 Taco-to-Go

 Missing Dart

 Ticket Taker

 Fish Dinner for Two

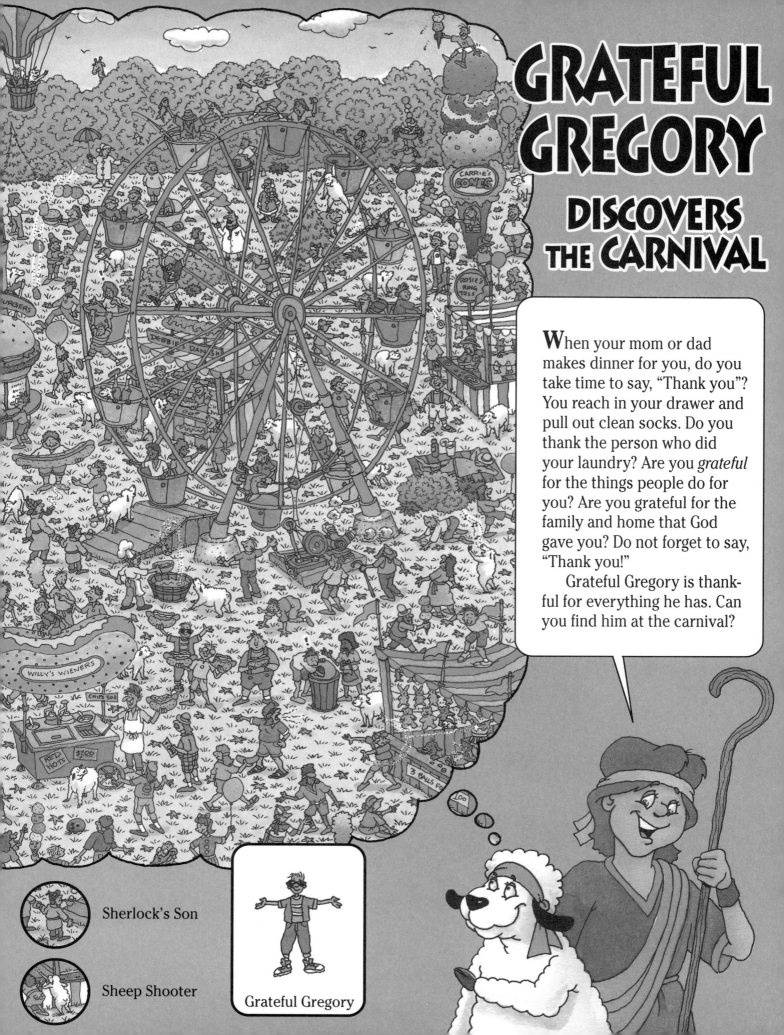

GRATEFUL GREGORY
DISCOVERS THE CARNIVAL

When your mom or dad makes dinner for you, do you take time to say, "Thank you"? You reach in your drawer and pull out clean socks. Do you thank the person who did your laundry? Are you *grateful* for the things people do for you? Are you grateful for the family and home that God gave you? Do not forget to say, "Thank you!"

Grateful Gregory is thankful for everything he has. Can you find him at the carnival?

Sherlock's Son

Sheep Shooter

Grateful Gregory

Find Sammy, the Shepherd, and as many of these things as you can.

 Cherry Picker

 Rocket Man

 Fast Food

 Up, Up, and Away

MOUNT SINAI

Moses climbed to the top of Mount Sinai because God had a special message to give him. God wrote the Ten Commandments telling His people how to live. He engraved them in stone with His finger.

God's commandments:

1. God should be first in your life.
2. Worship only God, not any kind of idol.
3. Do not take God's name in vain.
4. Remember God's Sabbath.
5. Treat your parents with respect.
6. Do not murder.
7. Do not commit adultery.
8. Do not steal.
9. Do not lie.
10. Do not covet what other people have.

Wrong Place, Wrong Time

A Little off the Top

Find Sammy, the Shepherd, and as many of these things as you can.

 Very Big Basket

 Strong Baby

 Giant Salt Shaker

 Smiling Rock

THE EXODUS

—Exodus 7–12

The Hebrew people had been slaves in Egypt for many, many years. They kept crying out to God for help. God sent Moses to tell the Egyptian king, Pharaoh, to let the Hebrew people go to another land. Not until ten terrible plagues wrecked the land, animals, and Egyptians did Pharaoh free the Hebrews. Then Moses led the six hundred thousand fighting men (add to that number all the women, children, and men who were not strong) out of Egypt.

We call this event the Exodus.

Police Officer

Singing Trio

Find Sammy, the Shepherd, and as many of these things as you can.

 Sheep Catching Oranges

 Red Balloon

 Burger Man

 Squirrel on Swing

JESUS BY THE SEA OF GALILEE

—Matthew 4:18-20; Mark 3:7-11;
Luke 5:4-6

Jesus often walked along the shore near the Sea of Galilee. Hundreds of people came out from the villages to hear Him teach. Many of them were sick or blind or crippled and wanted Jesus to heal them. He was always loving, kind, and patient with these people.

Jesus did all sorts of things by the sea. He helped the disciples catch fish there. He also called men to follow Him there. The people who loved Jesus had good memories of times spent with Him near the sea.

Water Fountain Man

Man in Cool Shades

Find Sammy, the Shepherd, and as many of these things as you can.

 Tree Topper

 Traveling Salesman

 Slingshot

 Pan Fish

FAITHFUL FREDDIE
ENJOYS DOWNHILL SKIING

Good friends are *faithful*. That means you can count on them. Faithful people say nice things about their friends when their friends are not around. They stick with their buddies even when their buddies hurt their feelings.

Faithful people make new friends without forgetting their old ones. You can trust a loyal, faithful friend.

Faithful Freddie told some friends he would meet them on the slopes. Can you find him there?

Real Hands–On Skier

Magic Carpet Ride

Faithful Freddie

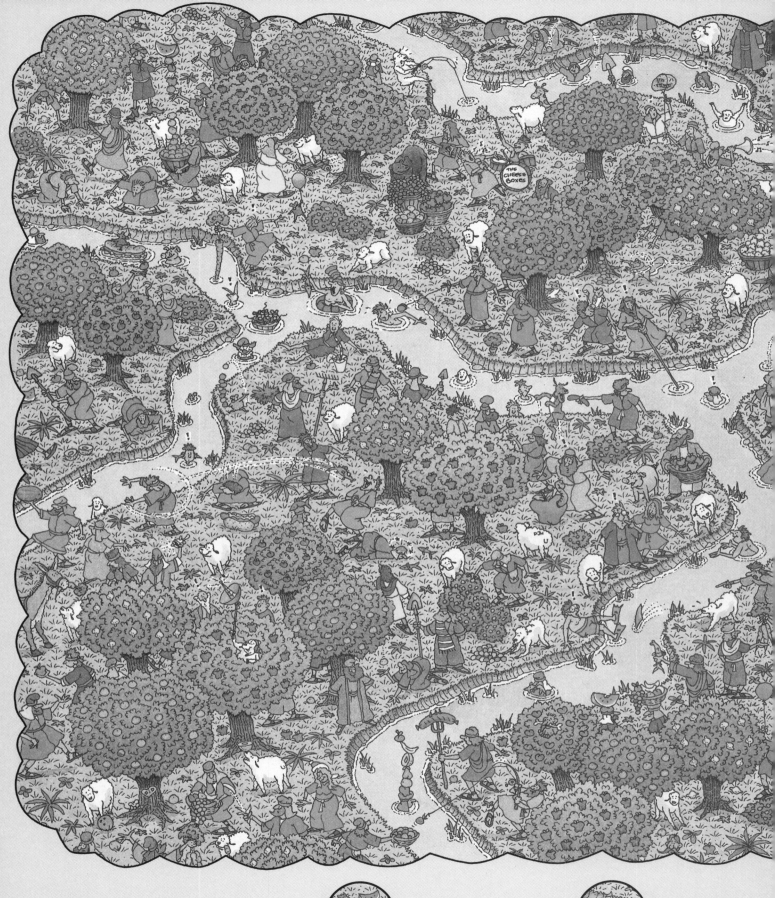

Find Sammy, the Shepherd, and as many of these things as you can.

 Hit It

 Soggy Sub

 Sounds Fishy to Me

 Wool Sweater

CANAAN

Canaan was the land that God had promised to give His people. The Hebrew people had been slaves in Egypt for a long time. They constantly asked God to make them free.

So God chose Moses to lead the Hebrews out of Egypt and to Canaan, the Promised Land. God performed many miracles to help them, but they still complained about little things. God punished them by keeping them from going into the Promised Land. The Hebrews wandered in the wilderness for over forty years.

Finally they came to the edge of Canaan. It was a beautiful country filled with many kinds of fruits and grains. The people who lived in Canaan were very big, and some of the Hebrews were frightened. God was disappointed in the people because they did not trust Him. In fact, He said that most of them would die without entering the Promised Land. But the children of those people grew up and trusted God to do what He said He would do. God helped them, and soon they were happily settled in their new land.

Sheep Dishing It Out

Beard Bout

Find Sammy, the Shepherd, and as many of these things as you can.

 Pot of Gold Coins

 Hungry Lamb

 Man Jumping Off Rock

 Baby in Diapers

THE GOLDEN CALF

—*Exodus 32*

Moses left the wandering Hebrews to go up the mountain to receive orders from God. While he was gone the people became restless. They went to Aaron, Moses' brother, and insisted that he make a god to lead them.

The people gave their gold to Aaron. He melted it down and formed it into an idol that looked like a calf.

The Hebrews were bowing down and dancing before the golden calf when Moses returned.

Moses saw what they were doing and became very angry. He burned the idol and ground it into powder. Then he scattered the powder on the water and made the people drink it.

Woman Plugging Her Ears

Man Doing Handstand on Sheep

Find Sammy, the Shepherd, and as many of these things as you can.

 Fish Sandwich

 Fish Heads

 Man in Tree

 Skipped Fish

JESUS FEEDS A HUNGRY CROWD

—Luke 9:11-17; John 6:1-14

Jesus had been teaching all day. Thousands of people had come to hear Him talk about God's kingdom. Now it was supper time, and the disciples thought Jesus should send the people away to eat.

But Jesus had a better idea. He had the disciples search through the crowd for anyone with food. They found one boy who had brought a lunch of five loaves of bread and two small fish. The little boy was happy to give his food to Jesus.

Jesus took the food and blessed it. Then the disciples passed it out to the crowd. More than five thousand people ate all they wanted that day, and there were even leftovers!

Bread and Butter

Balanced Diet

Find Sammy, the Shepherd, and as many of these things as you can.

 Is That My Ball?

 You'll Be Sorry

 Strong Shoes

 High Tech Golf

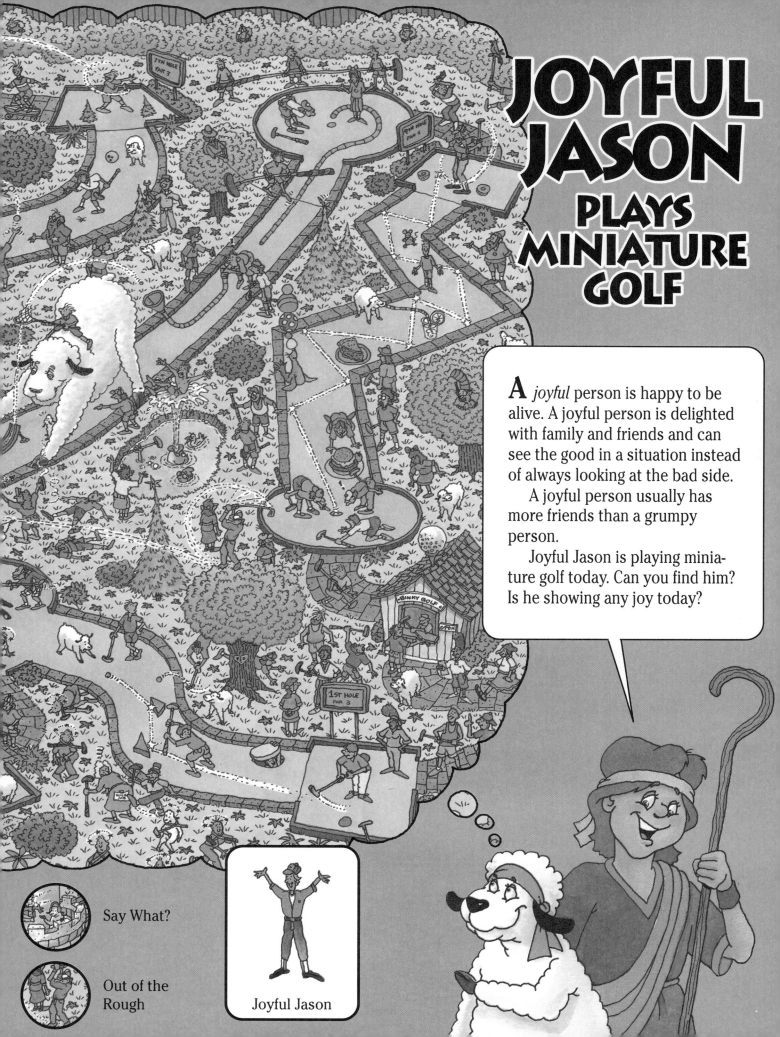

JOYFUL JASON
PLAYS MINIATURE GOLF

A *joyful* person is happy to be alive. A joyful person is delighted with family and friends and can see the good in a situation instead of always looking at the bad side.

A joyful person usually has more friends than a grumpy person.

Joyful Jason is playing miniature golf today. Can you find him? Is he showing any joy today?

Say What?

Out of the Rough

Joyful Jason

Find Sammy, the Shepherd, and as many of these things as you can.

Grape Wham

Funny Bunny

Radio Controlled

Out of Lunch

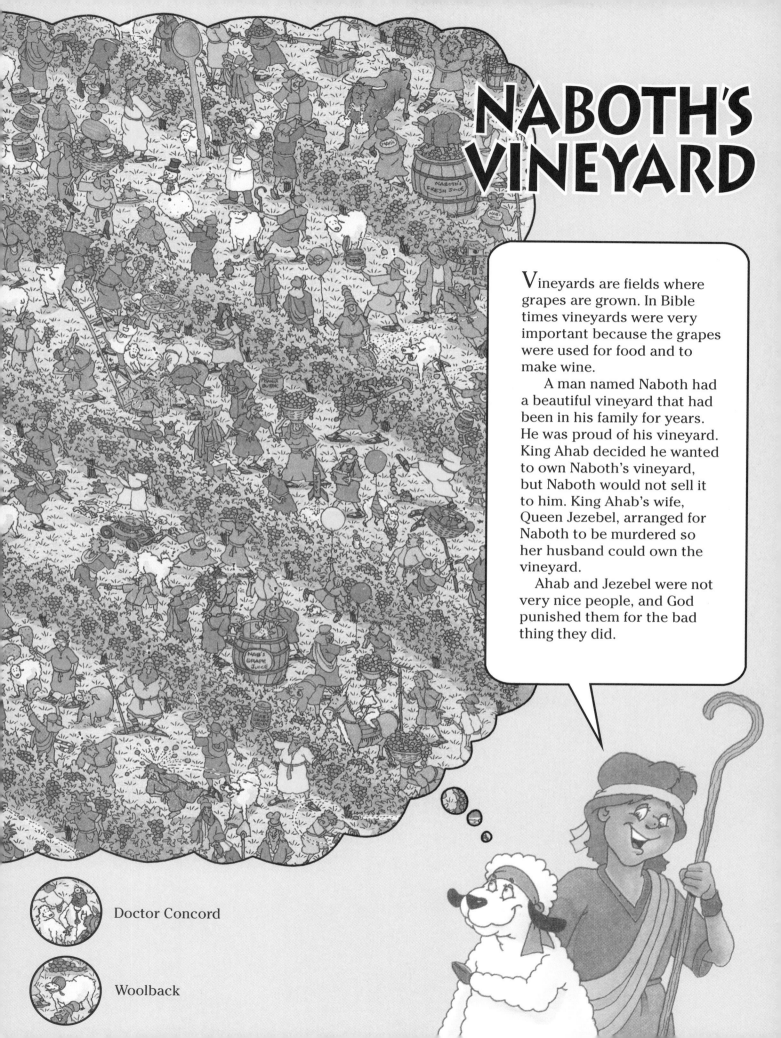

NABOTH'S VINEYARD

Vineyards are fields where grapes are grown. In Bible times vineyards were very important because the grapes were used for food and to make wine.

A man named Naboth had a beautiful vineyard that had been in his family for years. He was proud of his vineyard. King Ahab decided he wanted to own Naboth's vineyard, but Naboth would not sell it to him. King Ahab's wife, Queen Jezebel, arranged for Naboth to be murdered so her husband could own the vineyard.

Ahab and Jezebel were not very nice people, and God punished them for the bad thing they did.

Doctor Concord

Woolback

Find Sammy, the Shepherd, and as many of these things as you can.

 Snoozer

 Diver

 Sunbather

 Big Pencil

THE BATTLE OF JERICHO

—Joshua 6

God gave Joshua special instructions to defeat the enemy at Jericho.

God told Joshua to have all his men march around the city once each day for six days. On the seventh day they were to march around the city seven times. Then the priests were to blow rams' horns, and the men were to shout. Joshua probably thought the plan was strange, but he obeyed God anyway.

God kept His word and the walls came tumbling down.

Plate of Eggs

Soldier with Sling Shot

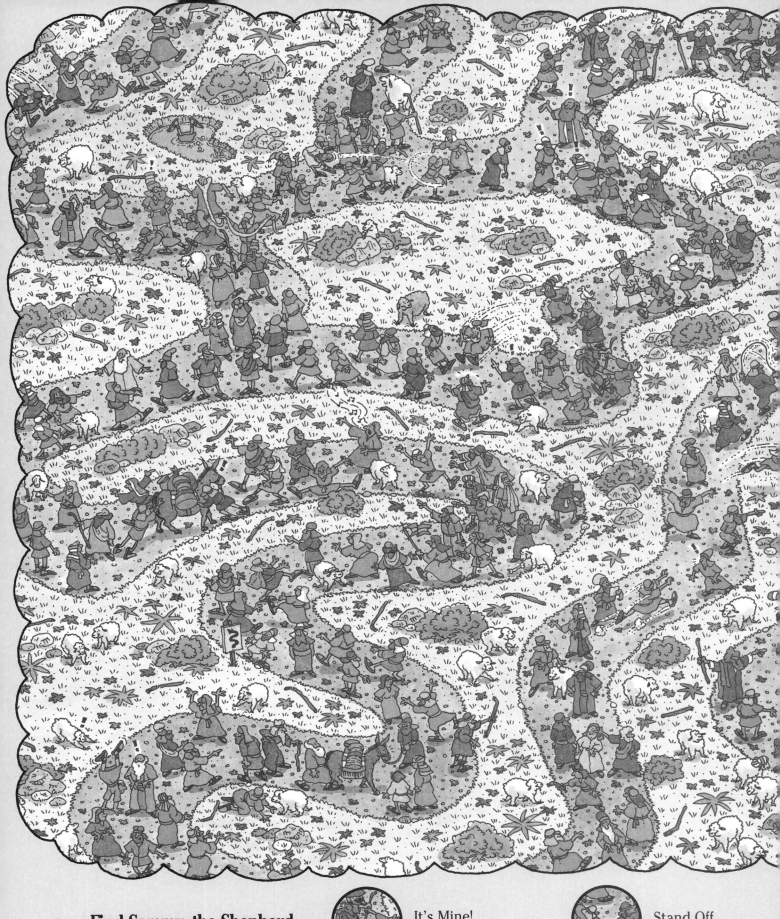

Find Sammy, the Shepherd, and as many of these things as you can.

 It's Mine!

 Stand Off

 Bread Thrower

 Short Cut

A MAN IN A TREE

—Luke 19:1-8

One time Jesus was passing through Jericho where a man named Zacchaeus lived. Zacchaeus was a tax collector, and sometimes he took more money than he should have from people. Zacchaeus wanted to see the teacher he had heard so much about. But he had a problem—he was a short man, and crowds of people lined the streets. He would never be able to see over them, and no one would let him through.

Suddenly Zacchaeus noticed a sycamore tree next to the road. That gave him an idea! He climbed the tree and had a bird's-eye view of Jesus coming down the road. When Jesus passed by, He called, "Zacchaeus, make haste and come down, for today I must stay at your house."

After Jesus and Zacchaeus talked for a while, Zacchaeus decided to give half his goods to the poor and to pay back four times what he owed to anyone from whom he had stolen.

Hot Dog Snack

Very Long Beard

Find Sammy, the Shepherd, and as many of these things as you can.

 Jammin' Sheep

 Water–Ski Mouse

 Sand Surfer

 Message in a Bottle

DILIGENT DANNY
GETS THE JOB DONE AT THE BEACH

When you are cleaning your room, emptying trash cans for your mom, doing homework, or working a puzzle, you should do your best to finish the project. That means you are being diligent.

Diligence is sticking with something until you have finished the project, even if it takes a long time. Finally finishing a hard puzzle is very satisfying.

Look at the picture of kids playing at the beach. My friend Diligent Danny is at the beach today. See if you can find him finishing a project.

No Snow

Bad Bump

Diligent Danny

Find Sammy, the Shepherd, and as many of these things as you can.

 Flutist

 Fresh Fish Sandwich

 High Wire Wash

 Sharpshooter

NAZARETH

Nazareth was a small, unimportant village in Galilee. Some people said that nothing good could come out of Nazareth. But someone very special grew up there.

After Jesus was born in Bethlehem, an angel told Joseph to take his little family to Egypt. A bad king wanted to kill baby Jesus. When the bad king died, the angel said that Joseph, Mary, and Jesus could go home to Nazareth.

Jesus grew up there with His family. Joseph taught Him how to be a carpenter like he was. Jesus had chores to do, and He played with His friends. In some ways, Jesus seemed like any other boy, but He was very different. He was the Son of God.

Exterminator

Fore

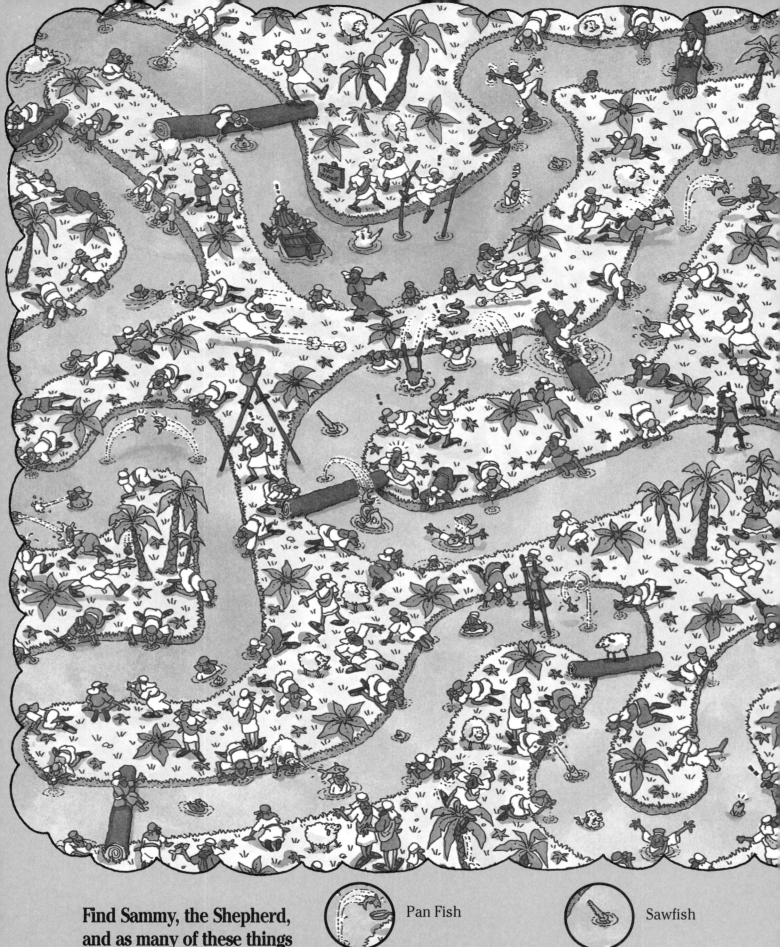

Find Sammy, the Shepherd, and as many of these things as you can.

 Pan Fish

Sawfish

 Skunk

 Snoozer

GENERAL GIDEON

—*Judges 7*

Gideon, God's chosen leader, was preparing for battle with the enemies of the Israelites.

God said to Gideon, "You have too many men. The people might think they won the victory all by themselves. Send home all who are afraid." Gideon did as God said, but he still had ten thousand men.

God told Gideon to have all the men go to the stream. He was to send home all who got down on both knees to drink.

Only three hundred men were left. God gave them the victory over a much larger number of enemy soldiers. Everyone knew that it was God's victory and that God was with Gideon.

Midair Collision

Floating Fish

Find Sammy, the Shepherd, and as many of these things as you can.

 Man on a Swing

 Tree Climber

 Sheep with a View

 Bird Man

JESUS RIDES INTO JERUSALEM

—Mark 11:1-10

Jesus and His disciples had been walking for many days, and now they were near Jerusalem. But Jesus stopped along the road and sent two disciples on an errand. He asked them to go into a nearby village. They would find a donkey colt tied there. They were to borrow the colt for Him to ride.

The disciples brought the colt to Jesus, and He rode it toward Jerusalem. Crowds of people lined the streets and waved palm branches as He rode by. Some even laid their coats down on the road in front of Jesus. The people followed Him to the city shouting, "Hosanna! Blessed is He who comes in the name of the LORD! . . . Hosanna in the highest!"

3 Peeking Sheep

Man on a Ladder

Find Sammy, the Shepherd, and as many of these things as you can.

 Unplugged

 Spare Ribs

 Not a Happy Camper

 Man with Taco

PATIENT PETER

WAITS HIS TURN AT THE CAMP FIRE

Waiting is hard. It is hard to wait for your friends to play the game you want to play. It is hard to wait your turn at the water fountain. It is even hard to wait for your parents to listen to what you want to tell them. When people are good at waiting, we call them *patient*.

Patient Peter has learned to wait. He is being patient at the camp fire. Can you find him?

Char Dog

Tune A. Fish

Patient Peter

Find Sammy, the Shepherd, and as many of these things as you can.

 Twin Mice

 Pan Fish

 Rodeo Rodent

 Sammy Seeker

THE WILDERNESS

A wilderness is a place where plants grow wild and not many people live. It may be a thick forest, or it may be a desert.

John the Baptist lived in the desert wilderness in Judea, not far from the Dead Sea. He wore clothes made from camel hair, and he ate locusts and wild honey.

John traveled around telling people that Jesus was coming. The message he gave helped the people get ready to hear what Jesus would tell them.

Photographer

Rocket Roller

Find Sammy, the Shepherd, and as many of these things as you can.

 Cannonball Lamb

 Bird with Flag

 Yelling Lamb

 Sunbather

DAVID AND GOLIATH

—1 Samuel 17

The Philistine armies were ready for a battle with Israel's armies. The Philistines had a champion—a nine-foot-tall giant named Goliath. He stood before his armies and yelled at the Israelites, "Send your best man to fight me. If he kills me, we will be your servants. If not, you will be our servants." No one in Israel's armies would take the challenge.

David, a shepherd boy, had come near the battle lines to bring food to his brothers. He heard Goliath defying the armies of Israel, and he was outraged. David said that he would fight the giant. God had helped David before, and he knew God would help him again.

That day God used David's sling and one smooth stone to kill the mighty Goliath.

Hungry Dog Jumping

Bird in Pain

Find Sammy, the Shepherd, and as many of these things as you can.

 Smooching Sheep

 Singing Soldier

 Camera Bug

 2-Spear Soldier

JESUS IS BETRAYED

—Mark 14:32-46

Jesus knew that His time on earth was nearly over. He took some of His disciples to the Garden of Gethsemane. He needed to pray, and He wanted His friends to be close by. All of the disciples were there except Judas.

While Jesus was speaking with His disciples, a crowd came into the garden carrying swords and clubs. Judas was leading them. He walked right up to Jesus and kissed Him on the cheek. This kiss was a signal for the others in the crowd, and they grabbed Jesus and arrested Him.

Pizza Man

Sheep in Shades

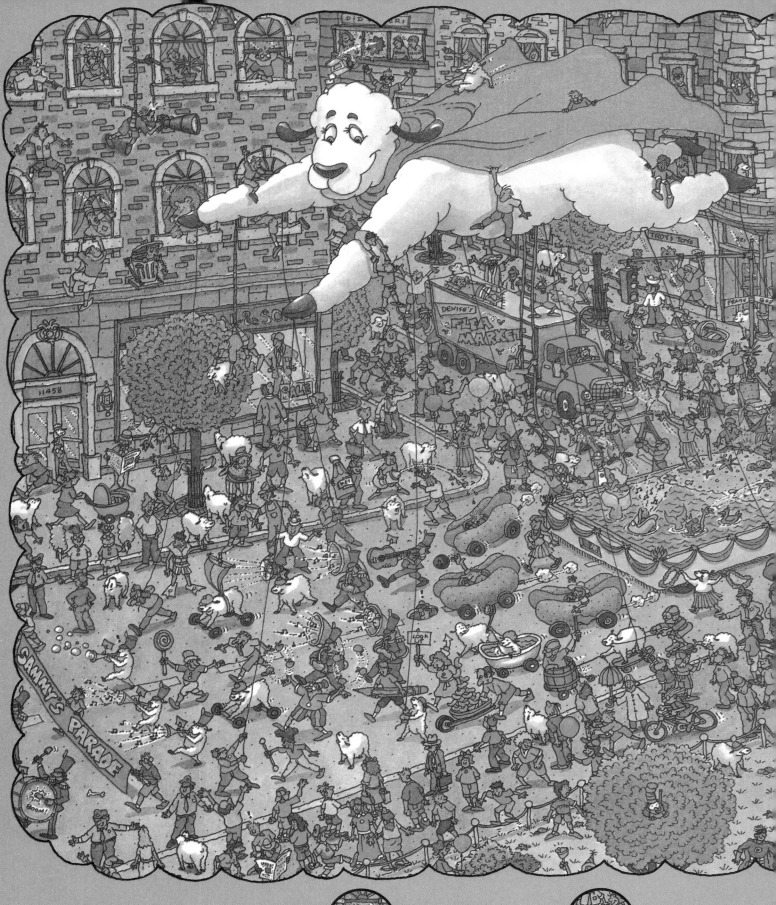

Find Sammy, the Shepherd, and as many of these things as you can.

 Emergency Phone Call

 Amateur Musician

 One Little Piggy

 Bold Boxer Shorts

HUMBLE HANNA
JOINS THE PARADE

Do you know people who are really smart or who have beautiful singing voices? If they brag about how good they are, you might not enjoy being around them. If they do not brag, they are being *humble*. Humble people do not tell you how great they are. Humble people do not mind if others are praised or cheered. They are just happy to do what they do and enjoy it.

Humble Hanna never brags. Today she is in a parade. When you find her, you might notice that she is being humble.

Light Lunch

Abe the Sheep

Humble Hanna

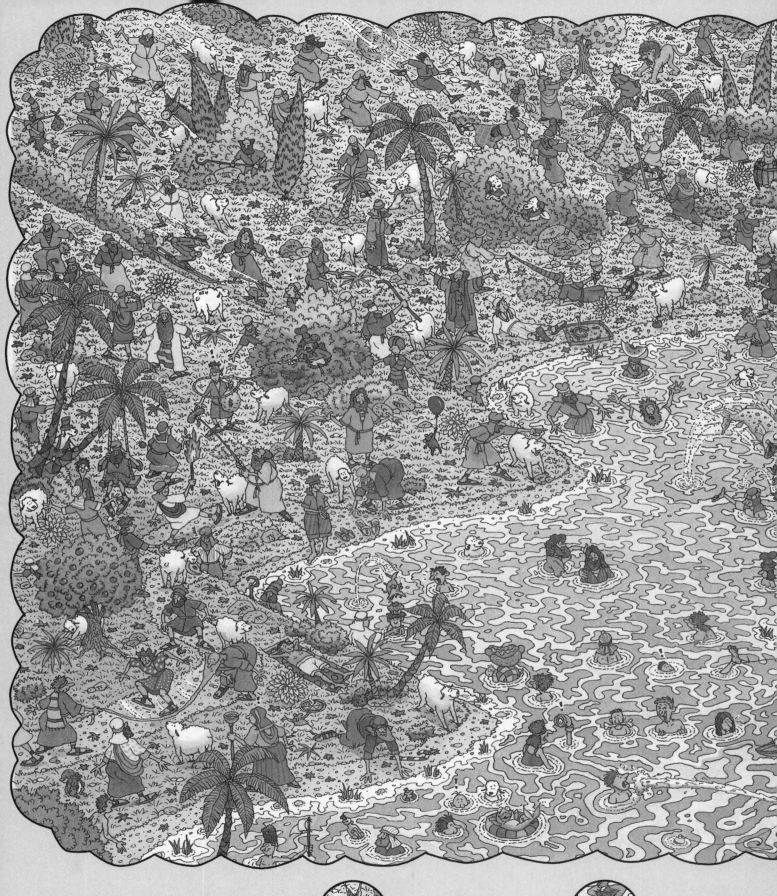

Find Sammy, the Shepherd, and as many of these things as you can.

 Party Animals

 Bob

 Suspendered Sheep

 Floating Fish

THE JORDAN RIVER

The Jordan River is the longest river in Palestine. Many important Bible events took place in or around the Jordan River.

John the Baptist was at the Jordan River teaching people about the Messiah who would come to save people from their sins. When a person believed in the Messiah, John baptized him in the Jordan River.

Jesus came and asked John to baptize Him. John knew this man was the Messiah and that Jesus should baptize him instead. But John did baptize Jesus because Jesus said that it was the right thing to do. Then God spoke from heaven saying, "This is My beloved Son, in whom I am well pleased."

Splitting Hairs

Horseshoe Headache

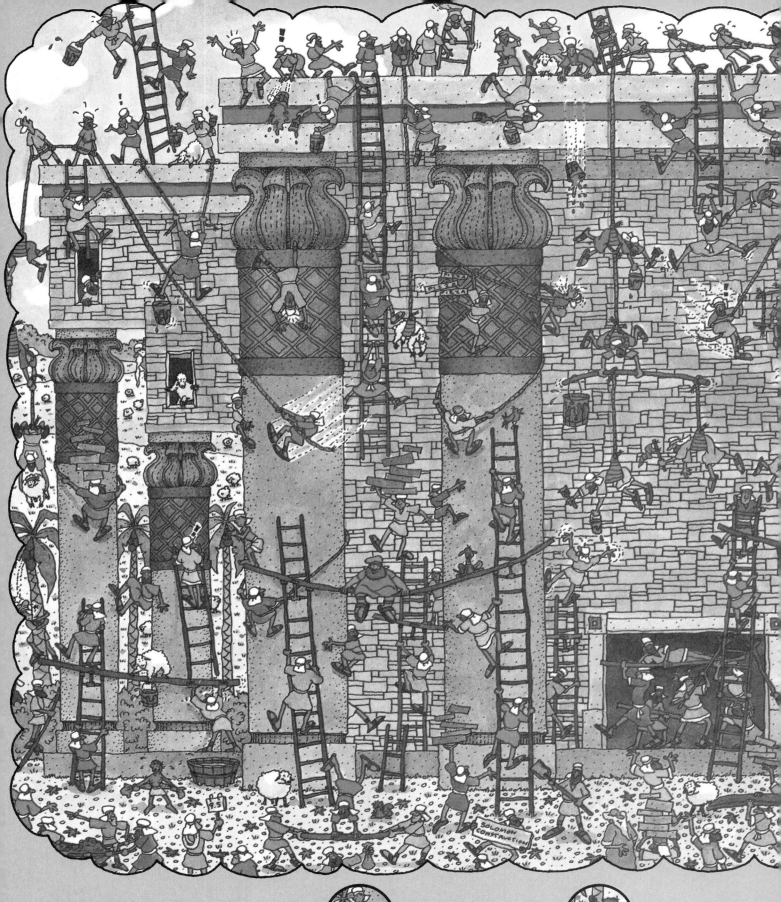

Find Sammy, the Shepherd, and as many of these things as you can.

 Diver

 Monkey

 Falling Paint Bucket

 Painting Sheep

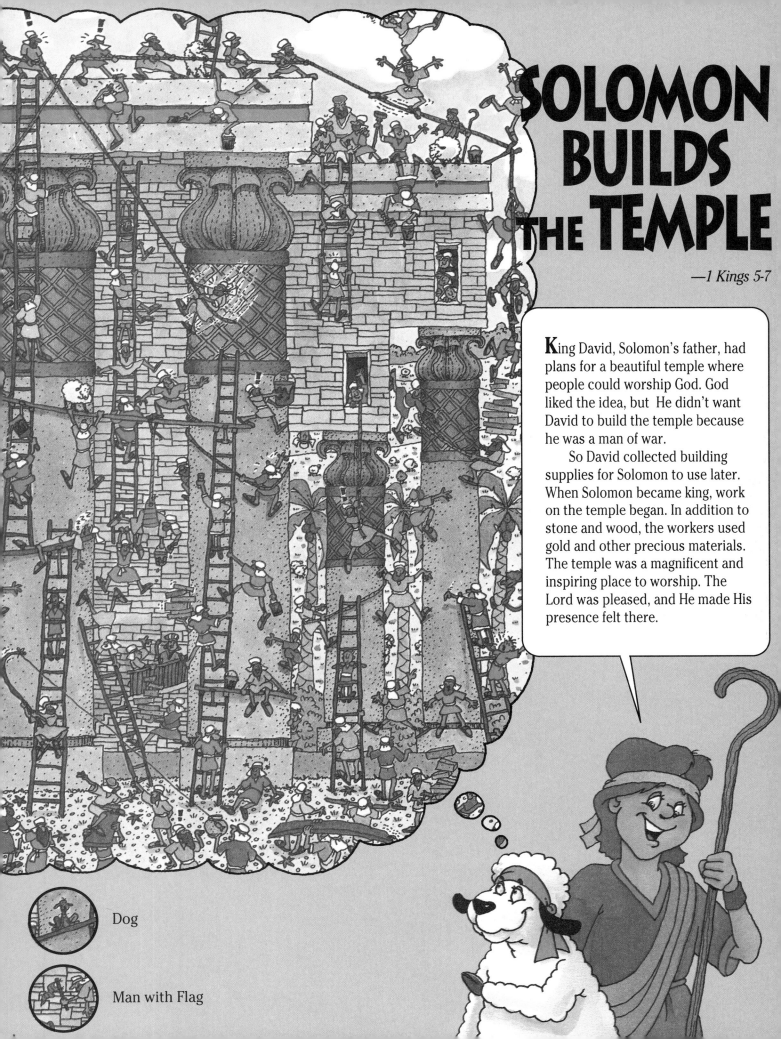

SOLOMON BUILDS THE TEMPLE

—1 Kings 5-7

King David, Solomon's father, had plans for a beautiful temple where people could worship God. God liked the idea, but He didn't want David to build the temple because he was a man of war.

So David collected building supplies for Solomon to use later. When Solomon became king, work on the temple began. In addition to stone and wood, the workers used gold and other precious materials. The temple was a magnificent and inspiring place to worship. The Lord was pleased, and He made His presence felt there.

Dog

Man with Flag

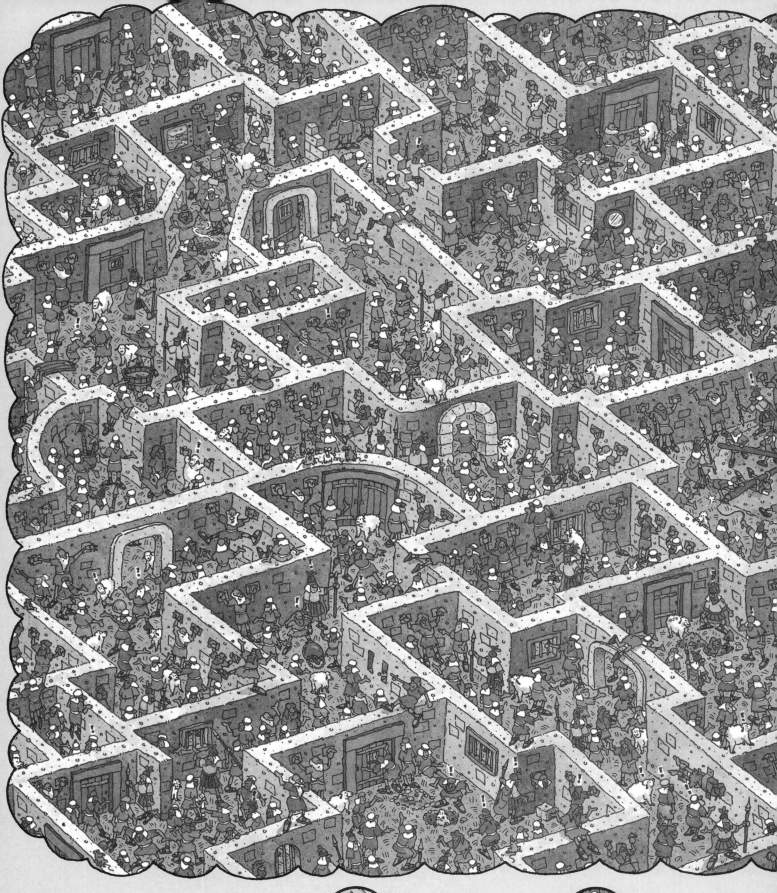

Find Sammy, the Shepherd, and as many of these things as you can.

 Side–Mounted Man

 Sheep with Ball and Chain

 3 Blind Mice

 Shirtless Soldier

PAUL AND SILAS IN JAIL

—Acts 16:16-34

Paul and Silas were in jail because they had cast a spirit out of a slave girl who told fortunes. The Romans were so angry with them that they beat them and put them in an inner cell. They didn't take any chances on Paul and Silas escaping.

Paul and Silas sang hymns and prayed that night as the other prisoners listened. Suddenly, around midnight, the floor and the walls began to shake. A strong earthquake shook the doors open, and the chains fell off all the prisoners. The jailer thought all his prisoners had escaped, and he started to kill himself. Paul stopped him by shouting, "Do yourself no harm, for we are all here."

The jailer was so impressed that he asked Paul and Silas how to be saved. They told him to believe in Jesus, and that very night the jailer and his whole family were baptized.

Small Door

Upside-Down Prisoner

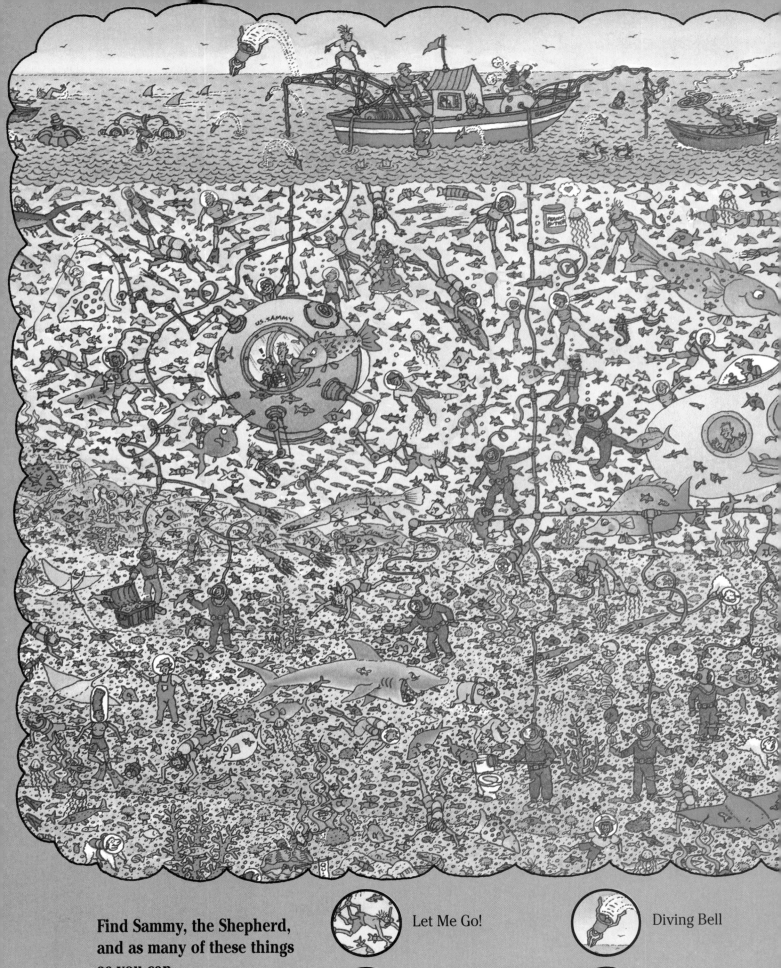

Find Sammy, the Shepherd, and as many of these things as you can.

Let Me Go!

Diving Bell

Scuba Cowboy

Coffee Break

COURTEOUS COURTNEY GOES SCUBA DIVING

Being *courteous* means being polite. For example, a courteous person takes turns on the playground swings. A courteous person says, "Excuse me," "Please," and "May I?" A courteous person does not run or shout inside buildings.

Courteous Courtney loves scuba diving. But even when she is doing her favorite thing, she remembers to be courteous. Can you find her?

Wrong Place, Wrong Time

Lunch Selection

Courteous Courtney

Find Sammy, the Shepherd, and as many of these things as you can.

 Roll for a Rodent

 Slingshot Sheep

 Fast Fish

 Foul Fish

GALILEE

One afternoon Jesus was teaching on a hillside in Galilee. More than five thousand people came out of the towns in the area to hear what He was teaching.

Jesus taught for many hours. The disciples said that He should send the people into the villages to eat dinner. But Jesus had a different idea. He wanted the disciples to feed the people. Of course, they did not have enough food to feed so many people. So Jesus took care of the problem.

Jesus asked if anyone in the crowd had food. One small boy had a lunch of five loaves of bread and two fish. Jesus took this small lunch, asked God's blessing, and fed all the people with it. The disciples even filled twelve baskets with what was left over! Everyone was amazed.

Three Men in a Tub

Cold Lamb

Find Sammy, the Shepherd, and as many of these things as you can.

 Picnic Basket

 Bird

 Striped Flag

 Swimming Hole

ELIJAH

—1 Kings 18

Elijah was a prophet of God. He challenged the prophets of Baal, a false god, to a showdown. Once and for all, he wanted to prove to the Israelites which God was real.

The prophets of Baal agreed to the test. They built their altar and then called and called and called on Baal to send down fire. Nothing happened.

Elijah built his altar, soaked the wood on it with water, and called on God to send down fire. The fire that flashed from heaven burned the wood and even the stones of the altar!

Man with Shovel

Old Man with Sunglasses

Find Sammy, the Shepherd, and as many of these things as you can.

 Strong Man

 Stick–Em–Up

 Woman with Bird

 Bar–B–Q

PAUL SPEAKS IN ATHENS

—*Acts 17:16-32*

Paul was in Athens teaching about Jesus, and he noticed that the people there worshiped strange gods instead of the one true God. He talked with some of the people about this, and they invited him to go to the Areopagus—a hill where they met— to speak with the council.

When Paul spoke there he said, "Men of Athens, I perceive that in all things you are very religious; for as I was passing through and considering the objects of your worship, I even found an altar with this inscription: TO THE UNKNOWN GOD. Therefore, the One whom you worship without knowing, Him I proclaim to you . . . Lord of heaven and earth."

The men of the council listened to Paul speak, and when he was finished, some of them asked to hear more about God.

Tightrope Walker

Bread Kicker

Find Sammy, the Shepherd, and as many of these things as you can.

 Motor Mouse

 Rocket Racer

 Fishin' Fool

 Ewe-nicycle

HELPFUL HENRY LENDS A HAND AT THE GO-CART TRACK

Are you good at putting model airplanes together? Can you French-braid hair? Are you better than anyone else at hitting a baseball? If a friend asks for your help with something that you do better than she does, are you willing to do it?

Each of us has a specialty, something that we enjoy doing and are good at. It is fun to be able to *help* a friend do something. You feel needed, and your friend is grateful for your help.

Helpful Henry has a specialty. He is busy at the go-cart track right now using his specialty to help someone. Can you find him?

Ironic Chores

Out of Season

Helpful Henry

Find Sammy, the Shepherd, and as many of these things as you can.

 Ice Cream for Two

 Flower Girl

 Say What?

 Swiss Hotel

BETHANY

The small town of Bethany was the home of three of Jesus's special friends. Mary, Martha, and Lazarus—two sisters and a brother—played a big part in one of Jesus's most well-known miracles.

Lazarus was very sick, so his sisters sent for Jesus. They knew He could help their brother. But by the time Jesus arrived, Lazarus was dead.

Jesus knew that Mary, Martha, and Lazarus believed He was the Son of God. He went to the tomb of Lazarus and called for the dead man to come out. Lazarus walked out of the tomb, still wrapped in grave clothes. He was alive— and many people believed in Jesus that day!

Diver

Man with Paper Dolls

Find Sammy, the Shepherd, and as many of these things as you can.

 Baby in Diaper

 Fish in Mouth

 Man-Hole in Table

 Very Big Bone

MENE, MENE,
TEKEL, UPHARSIN.

AMAZING WRITING ON THE WALL

—Daniel 5

King Belshazzar and his many banquet guests were having a wild time. Suddenly human fingers appeared and wrote on a wall. The king was scared and puzzled.

None of his wise men could explain what the writing meant, so King Belshazzar sent for Daniel. Daniel said the writing meant Belshazzar would die, and the Medes and Persians would take over his kingdom. That's exactly what happened that very night.

Bone Bearded Man

Spotted Dog

Find Sammy, the Shepherd, and as many of these things as you can.

 Triple Scoopers

 Melon Man

 Hot Dogs

 Pizza Man

THE RIOT AT EPHESUS

—Acts 19:23-41

Paul and his friends were traveling around telling people to worship only the one true God—not the idols that were so popular. This made some people in Ephesus very angry.

One man named Demetrius made his living by building silver shrines of the goddess Diana. Demetrius began stirring up the people against Paul. He said Paul was going to ruin their businesses and take away their income. Soon the whole city was in an uproar. Two of Paul's companions were seized to be put on trial.

Finally the city clerk calmed the screaming crowd. He told Demetrius and the others that if they had a problem with Paul they should go to the courts. They could not take the law into their own hands.

Skateboard Man

Sticky Situation

Find Sammy, the Shepherd, and as many of these things as you can.

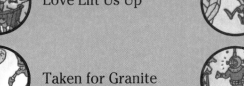

Love Lift Us Up

Light Snack

Taken for Granite

Sky Diver?

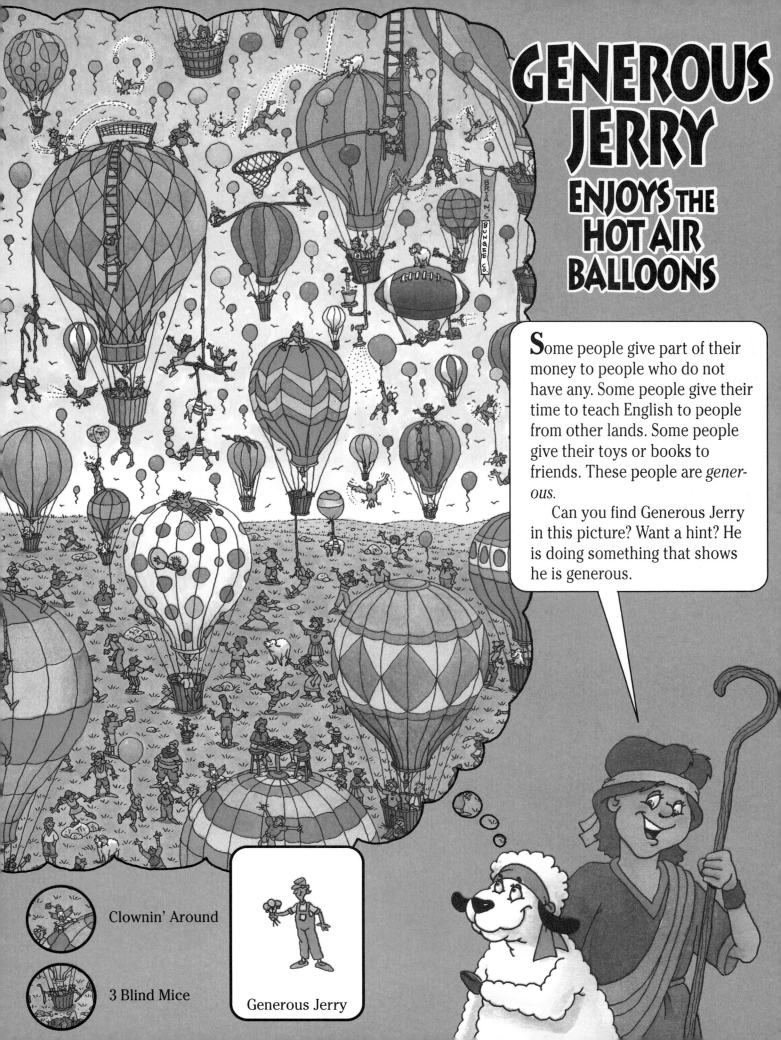

GENEROUS JERRY ENJOYS THE HOT AIR BALLOONS

Some people give part of their money to people who do not have any. Some people give their time to teach English to people from other lands. Some people give their toys or books to friends. These people are *generous.*

Can you find Generous Jerry in this picture? Want a hint? He is doing something that shows he is generous.

Clownin' Around

3 Blind Mice

Generous Jerry

Find Sammy, the Shepherd, and as many of these things as you can.

 Fowl Play

 Rat Roast

 William I'm Telling

 Chilly Willy

JERUSALEM

Jerusalem was a large city where many people lived. In Jerusalem there were many businesses and a large church, called a temple.

People went to the temple to worship God. They usually brought animals to give as sacrifices to God. Some people had started selling animals in the temple for a lot of money. Jesus went to the temple to worship and saw these people cheating the poor. He did not like that. So Jesus chased them out of the temple. He told them that God's house was a place to worship, not a place to make money.

Column Climber

Southwestern Sheep

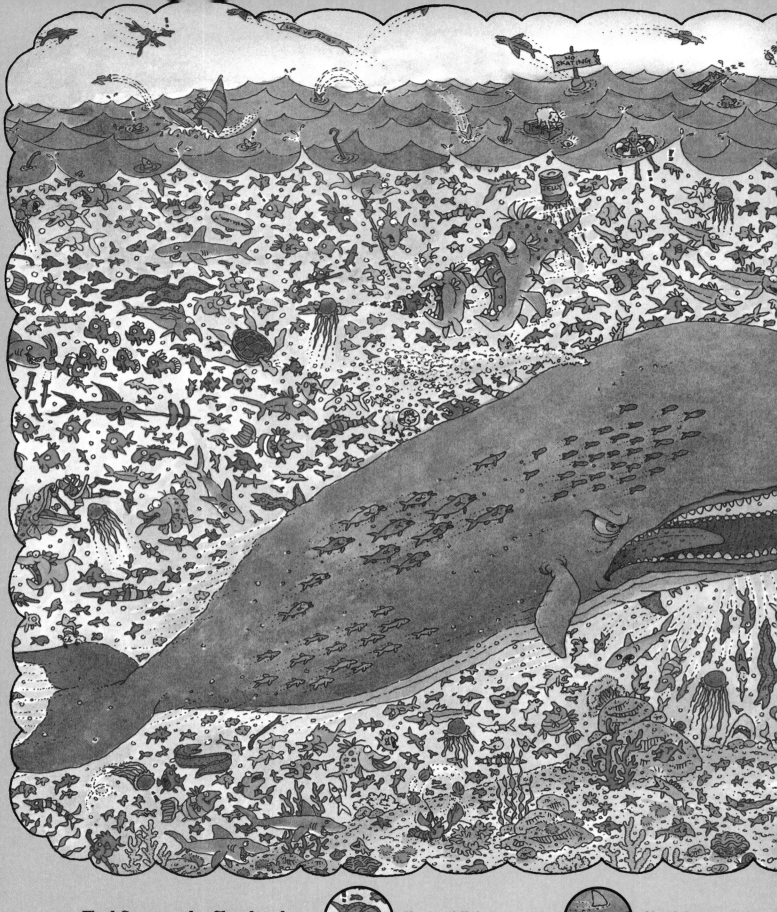

Find Sammy, the Shepherd, and as many of these things as you can.

 Knotted Eel

 Shark Imposter

 Blindfolded Fish

 Sawfish

JONAH'S LESSON

—Jonah

God told Jonah to go to Nineveh to preach against evil. Jonah did not want to, so he got on a ship going in the opposite direction.

A terrible storm blew up. Jonah knew it was storming because he had disobeyed God. He told the sailors to throw him overboard so the storm would stop. They did, and it did.

God had a huge fish swallow Jonah in one gulp. God had the fish spit him out on land three days later.

God again told Jonah to take His message to the people of Nineveh. This time Jonah obeyed.

Blimp Fish

Three Nail Fish

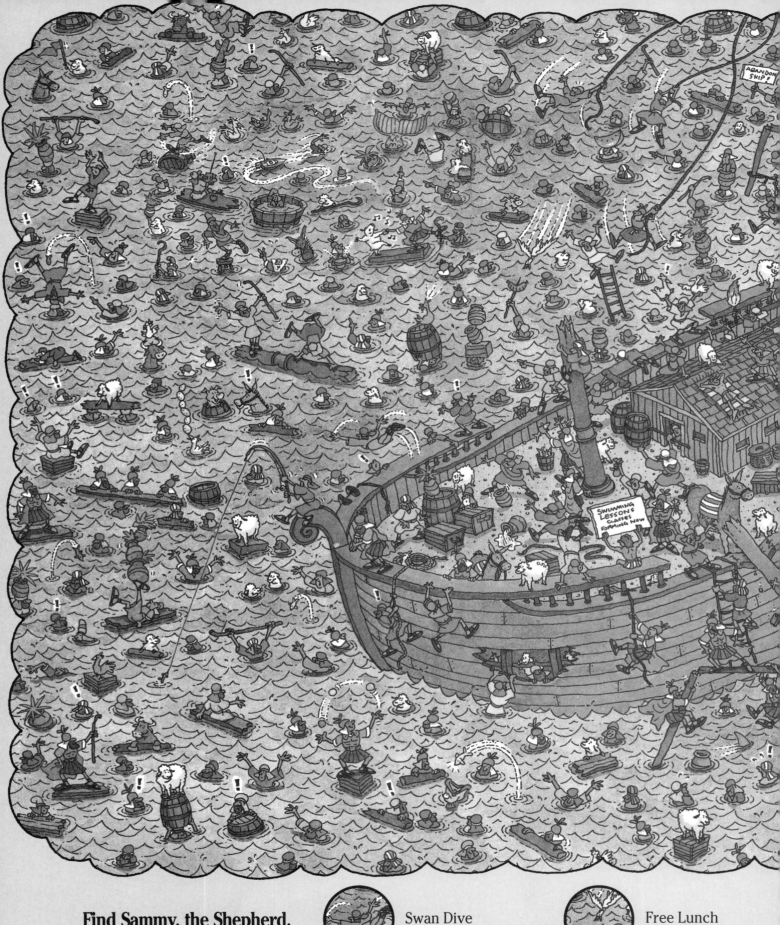

Find Sammy, the Shepherd, and as many of these things as you can.

 Swan Dive

 Free Lunch

Peaceful Old Man

Nice Catch

PAUL IS SHIPWRECKED

—*Acts 27:13-44*

Paul had been taken prisoner in Jerusalem, and he asked to be tried before Caesar in Rome. Now he and some other prisoners were on a ship that was sailing for Italy.

Before long, a terrible storm blew up. Some of the sailors were frightened and wanted to abandon ship. But Paul—with the soldiers' help—convinced everyone to stay and even to eat so they would be strong. The crew did as Paul said. Then they began to throw some things overboard to try to save the ship. But the ship ran aground that morning, and the strong waves began pounding it and breaking it into pieces.

Some of the soldiers wanted to kill the prisoners on board, but the centurion wouldn't let them. He wanted Paul to be safe. Instead everyone jumped overboard and swam or floated safely to shore.

Bad Balance

Seafood Snack

Find Sammy, the Shepherd, and as many of these things as you can.

 Shady Character

 Kitty Napped

 Souvenir Sheep

 Whistling Dickie

KIND CHRISTINA
SPENDS A DAY AT THE ZOO

A *kind* person is gentle and friendly. A kind person cares about others' feelings. You show kindness by the way you speak to your brother or sister. You show kindness by the way you treat your pets. You show kindness by your tone of voice when you speak with others. Kind people make others want to be kind.

Kind Christina is at the zoo. She is probably doing something that shows how kind she is. Can you find her?

The Muffin Man

Walkin' the Dog

Kind Christina

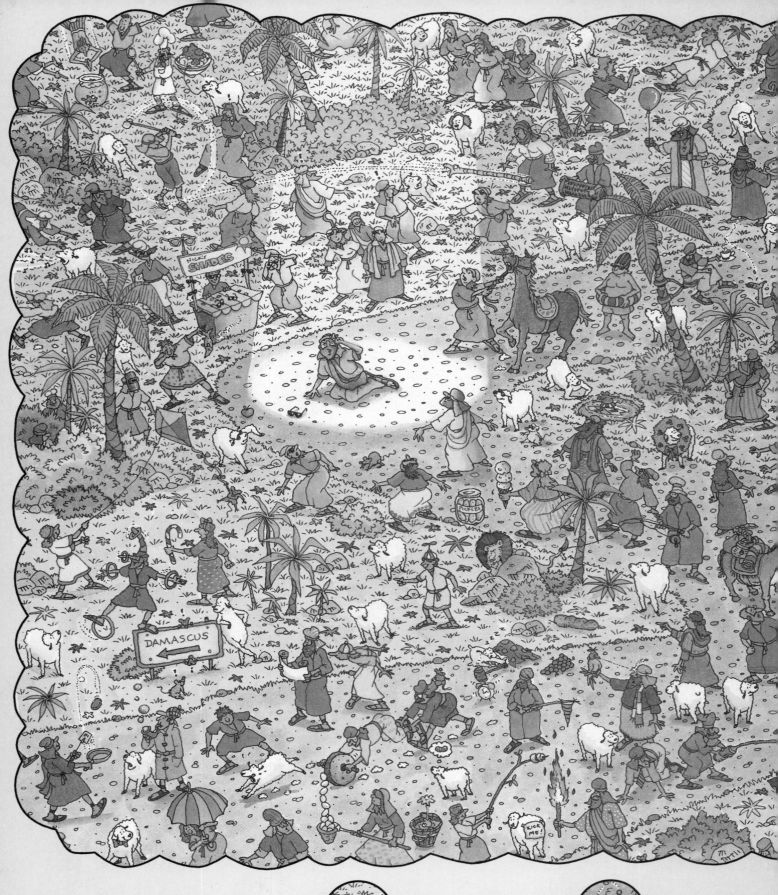

Find Sammy, the Shepherd, and as many of these things as you can.

 Angry Woman

 In the Spotlight

 Mouse Juggler

 Alien Mouse

THE DAMASCUS ROAD

Saul hated everyone who believed in Jesus. He tried to put Christians in jail and make them miserable in any way he could.

One day, Saul was on the Damascus Road. He had permission from the high priest to look for Christians in Damascus. Suddenly a bright light shone down on Saul, and he heard a voice. "Why are you persecuting Me, Saul?" the voice asked.

"Who are you?" Saul replied.

"I am Jesus, whom you are persecuting," the voice answered.

This convinced Saul that Jesus was really the Son of God and that He was alive. So Saul became a Christian. People started to call him Paul, and he spent the rest of his life telling people about Jesus. Paul wrote many books in the Bible.

Welder

Seed Shooter

SEEKING SAMMY

See how many crazy things you can find

IN THE GARDEN
1. Ramming Goat
2. Fisher
3. Smiling River
4. Snoozing Bear
5. Giraffe Trio
6. Rabbits Sharing Carrot
7. Two Camels—Three Humps
8. Convict Zebra
9. Sliding Giraffe
10. Water-Fun Monkey

THE SHEPHERDS SEE ANGELS
1. Strong Angel
2. Mouse Angel
3. Wiener Roaster
4. Radio
5. Bone
6. Chicken Drumstick
7. Angel Reading Book
8. Mouse
9. Upside–Down Angel
10. Wingless Angel
11. Angel in Sunglasses

COURAGEOUS CODY VISITS THE CIRCUS
1. Egg Thrower
2. Fish on Unicycle
3. Cowboy Clown
4. Dog
5. Sheep Family
6. Firefighter
7. Mouse Juggler
8. Bag of Peanuts
9. Sheep with Sunglasses
10. Native American Blowing Bubbles
11. Strong Mouse

MOUNT ARARAT
1. Knotted Snake
2. Roasted Marshmallow
3. Spider
4. Pail of Milk
5. Toaster
6. Necktie
7. Forked Tongue
8. Worm for Two
9. Piggy Bank
10. Sharkshooter
11. Porcupine Love

NOAH'S ARK
1. Bunch of Nuts
2. Ticklish Pig

3. Snoozing Giraffe
4. Butterfly Catcher
5. Juggling Seal
6. Dropped Bucket
7. Checkered Frog
8. Broken Board
9. Drying Laundry
10. White Giraffe
11. Water Hole

THE MISSING BOY
1. Bar of Soap
2. Birdhouse
3. Cross Country Skier
4. Sunbather
5. Lost Shorts
6. Money Sack
7. Man Slipping on Banana Peel
8. Sheep Walking Donkey
9. Spaghetti Man
10. Sledgehammer

SHARIN' KAREN HAS FUN AT THE PICNIC
1. Spaghetti and Meatballs
2. Mustard Gun
3. Alarm Clock
4. Mouse on Sub
5. Taco
6. Monkey with Banana
7. Corn Catcher
8. Ten–Foot Hot Dog
9. Giant Sundae
10. Bucket of Barbecue Sauce
11. Water Fountain

EGYPT
1. Taco
2. Baby with Bottle
3. Mouse Paratrooper
4. Cake Crusader
5. Three Blind Mice
6. Chicken Leg Lunch
7. Big Chili Pepper
8. Slave Driver
9. Ice Bucket
10. Candy Cane
11. Slice of Blueberry Pie

THE TOWER OF BABEL
1. Three-Person Elevator
2. Bowling
3. Three Upset Birds
4. Mismatched Door
5. Mouse Dropping Rock
6. Diving Board
7. Man Buried in Rock Pile

8. Skipping Ladder
9. Broken Ladder
10. Man with Chicken Leg

THE FIRST MIRACLE
1. Giraffe
2. Very Tall Man
3. Man Doing Cartwheel
4. Girl Twirling Baton
5. Man on Sled
6. Man in Barrel
7. Radio
8. Man in Manhole
9. Big Bowling Ball
10. Sunbather
11. Woman Reading Book

RUTH THE TRUTH RIDES THE WATERSLIDE
1. Man Reading Book
2. Rabbit
3. Mouse in Kayak
4. Smelly Sneaker
5. Giraffe
6. Fishbowl
7. Juggling Monkey
8. Boy on Hook
9. Lion
10. Umbrella
11. Donkey

THE RED SEA
1. Alarm Clock
2. Guitar Player
3. Brick Boat
4. Sailing Mouse
5. Birthday Cake
6. Television
7. Bride
8. Whistling Women
9. Surfing Mouse
10. Soccer Ball
11. Woman Flipping Coin

THE COLORFUL COAT
1. Fishing Lamb
2. Sheep Doing Cartwheel
3. Horse
4. Dog
5. Sheep with Staff in Mouth
6. Double-Hooked Staff
7. Sheep Pyramid
8. Two Dancing Sheep
9. Sheep Jumping Rope
10. Hats for Sale

A SICK MAN DROPS IN
1. Snorkeler
2. Loaf of Bread
3. Bird on Man's Shoulder
4. Kick–Me Sign
5. Smoochers
6. Hot Tea
7. Attractive Woman
8. Woman Holding Fish
9. Party Man
10. Cowboy

GRATEFUL GREGORY DISCOVERS THE CARNIVAL
1. Boy with Bubble Gum
2. Watermelon for Two
3. Three–Foot Hot Dog
4. Boom Box
5. Overdressed Man
6. Singing Sheep
7. Football Players
8. Man with Rocket Pack
9. Doughnut Balloon
10. Taco
11. Bone in Man's Beard

MOUNT SINAI
1. Fresh Grape Juice
2. Plunger
3. Sheep Police
4. Mouse House
5. Bird Nest
6. Fresh Milk
7. Firecracker
8. Alarm Clock
9. Miniature Christmas Tree
10. Inline Skater
11. Bird with Hat

THE EXODUS
1. Lemonade Stand
2. Snoozer
3. Five Person Train
4. Crowing Rooster
5. Juggler
6. Black Sheep
7. Skipping Rope
8. Woman with Two Flags
9. Choking Sheep
10. Man Carrying Three Rolls of Carpet

JESUS BY THE SEA OF GALILEE
1. Barrel of Monkeys
2. Man Holding Two Doves
3. Snake
4. Coconut Shaker
5. Woman Holding Fish
6. Man Giving Woman Flower
7. Ricochet Rock
8. Wind-Blown Hat
9. White Envelope
10. Man with Shovel
11. Book

FAITHFUL FREDDIE ENJOYS DOWNHILL SKIING
1. Frozen Fish
2. Runaway Bathtub
3. Three–Person Skis
4. Ski Boat
5. Rocket Man
6. Man on Inline Skates
7. Snow Cones for Sale
8. Flower Garden
9. Sunbather
10. Drummer on Skis
11. Book

CANAAN
1. Three Blind Mice
2. Giant Worm
3. Man with Bone
4. Rock Balloon
5. Giraffe
6. Crocodile
7. Fishy Phone Call
8. Ice Cream Sundae
9. Pond Patrol
10. Sailboat
11. Shark

THE GOLDEN CALF
1. Angry Moses
2. Burned Hot Dog
3. Juggler
4. Man Standing on Another Man's Shoulders
5. Snoozer
6. Four People Holding Hands
7. Bird
8. Huge Hot Dogs
9. Human Dominoes
10. Matador

JESUS FEEDS A HUNGRY CROWD
1. Five–Man Loaf
2. Two–Man Fish
3. Man Hiding in Basket
4. Sheep Throwing Bread
5. Fish Juggler
6. Snoozer
7. Shirtless Man
8. Man Balancing Three Baskets of Bread
9. Sheep in Basket
10. Sheep on Man's Back
11. Two–Point Bread

JOYFUL JASON PLAYS MINIATURE GOLF
1. Overdressed Man
2. Slice of Blueberry Pie
3. Firefighter
4. Woman with Very Long Hair
5. Bowler
6. Fruit Bowl Hat
7. Three–Person Putter
8. Tightrope Walker
9. Sunbather
10. Turtle
11. Manhole
12. Baby in Diaper

NABOTH'S VINEYARD
1. Iron
2. Pumpkin
3. Baby
4. Mice in Love
5. Mouse in Inner Tube
6. Indian
7. Can of Beans
8. Paper Airplane
9. Broken Shovel
10. Goldfish
11. Woman with Curly Cane

THE BATTLE OF JERICHO
1. Juggler
2. Sheep with Hat
3. Barbecue
4. Stretcher
5. Big Step
6. Cake
7. Game of Marbles
8. Two–Headed Spear
9. Pig
10. Blindfolded Soldier
11. Man Stuck in Roof

A MAN IN A TREE
1. Singing Woman
2. Z Stick
3. Two Men Pushing Donkey
4. Man Doing Splits
5. Hot Coffee
6. Sheep with Staff in Mouth
7. Snoozer
8. White Dove on Man's Head
9. Rope Skipper
10. Underwater Headstand
11. Woman with Flag

SEEKING SAMMY

See how many crazy things you can find

DILIGENT DANNY GETS THE JOB DONE AT THE BEACH
1. Flying Carpet
2. Lost Skaters
3. Toy Train
4. Blindfolded Head Bangers
5. Shark Imposters
6. Boom Box
7. Goat
8. Sheep Surfer
9. Man in Bath
10. Swordfish
11. Three Carrots

NAZARETH
1. Three Blind Mice
2. Snowman
3. Pied Piper
4. Sheep in Love
5. Man Snorkling
6. Giant Taco
7. Suitcase
8. Bird Man
9. Bird with Glasses
10. Vacuum
11. Mouse on Paper Plane

GENERAL GIDEON
1. Big Hungry Fish
2. Soldier in Tree
3. Broken Log Bridge
4. Fisher
5. Floating Lamb
6. Strong Soldier
7. Fish Juggler
8. "No Wake" Sign
9. Coconut Catcher
10. Fish on Soldier's Head
11. Two Soldiers Falling into River

JESUS RIDES INTO JERUSALEM
1. Singing Man
2. Clothesline
3. Pizza Man
4. Weather Vane
5. Bone
6. Man Selling Palms
7. Street Sign
8. Man Bowing Down on Knees
9. Very Long Beard
10. Man Standing on Stool
11. Falling Coconut

PATIENT PETER WAITS HIS TURN AT THE CAMP FIRE
1. Tightrope Mouse

2. Bucket of Wieners
3. Flying Bat
4. Hot Feet
5. Running Turtle
6. Mustard and Catsup
7. Handcuffed Hot Dogs
8. Mud Hole Man
9. Sub Sandwich
10. Football
11. Stinky Boots

THE WILDERNESS
1. Giant Pencil
2. Lawn Mower
3. Pasta for Four
4. Man with Mirror
5. Sawfish
6. Bomb
7. Beards Tied
8. Taco
9. Man
10. Sugar Cubes
11. Sheep Chef

DAVID AND GOLIATH
1. Fish
2. Tightrope Walker
3. Snoozer
4. Soldier Hiding in Tree
5. Sitting Horse
6. Bucking Lamb
7. Four–Person Spear
8. Lamb Riding Horse
9. Sunbathing Sheep
10. Soldier Sitting Backward on Horse

JESUS IS BETRAYED
1. Twin Torch
2. Golfer
3. Three–Man Spear
4. Sheep in Tree
5. Two–Headed Spear
6. Small Torch
7. Sheep Fountain
8. Soldier Roasting Wiener
9. Bone
10. Teeter–Totter

HUMBLE HANNA JOINS THE PARADE
1. Photographer
2. Cannonball Catcher
3. Sheep with Fan on Head
4. Bungee Jumper
5. Sheep Reading Book
6. Mustard Squirter
7. Man in Barrel

8. Man with Fog Mask
9. Sheep Blowing Bubbles
10. Pirate
11. Woman in Rollers

THE JORDAN RIVER
1. Message in Bottle
2. Cupcake–Eating Fish
3. Pizza Mouse
4. Ship Sheep
5. Woman Skipping Rocks
6. Bound Bandit
7. Downhill Skier
8. Tea for Two
9. Elephant Shower
10. Tight Tube

SOLOMON BUILDS THE TEMPLE
1. Pizza Delivery Person
2. Potential Collision
3. Two Men Getting Hands Stepped On
4. Dizzy Worker
5. Snoozer
6. Bird
7. Worker with Plunger
8. Very Heavy Man
9. Fisher
10. Surfer

PAUL AND SILAS IN JAIL
1. Very Long Beard
2. Tightrope Mouse
3. Prisoner Carrying Wood Box
4. Pizza Man
5. Wall–Shackled Sheep
6. Diver
7. Wall Clock
8. Snapped Whip
9. Bowling Ball
10. Sheep in Hole
11. Man Standing on Another Man's Shoulders

COURTEOUS COURTNEY GOES SCUBA DIVING
1. Mouse Sub
2. Two Thirsty Fish
3. Treasure Chest
4. Mermaid
5. Lobster Drummer
6. Peanut Butter and Jelly Love
7. Sawfish
8. Hot Dog Fish
9. Yelling Fish
10. Fishbowl
11. Two Bone Heads

GALILEE
1. Radio
2. Cleaning Woman
3. Native American
4. Mouse in Manhole
5. Astronaut
6. Surfer
7. Bowl of Cherries
8. Message in Bottle
9. Sheep in Shades
10. Roman Soldier
11. Sawfish

ELIJAH
1. Snake
2. Checkered Flag
3. Dog
4. Thrown Loaf of Bread
5. Man Kissing Stone
6. Two Steaks
7. Pig
8. Juggler
9. Roasting Marshmallows
10. Snoozer
11. Man Hiding in Tree

PAUL SPEAKS IN ATHENS
1. Barrel of Monkeys
2. Christmas Tree
3. Hot Cup of Coffee
4. Very Long Beard
5. Man on Unicycle
6. Pizza Man
7. Maps for Sale
8. Baseball Fan
9. Hot Dog on Stick
10. Man Throwing Frisbee
11. Tennis Racket

HELPFUL HENRY LENDS A HAND AT THE GO–CART TRACK
1. On Road Bath
2. Three–Person Car
3. Pit Stop
4. Ice Cream Bar
5. Inline Skater
6. Watermelon on Wheels
7. Umbrella
8. Spiderweb
9. Catsup Cart
10. Ten–Scoop Cone
11. Man with Binoculars

BETHANY
1. Violinist
2. Slice of Blueberry Pie
3. Boy with Bat
4. Two Brooms

5. Surprise Shower
6. Studious Sheep
7. Unicycle Mouse
8. Dinosaur
9. Jar of Pickles
10. Kite Flyer
11. Super Hero

AMAZING WRITING ON THE WALL
1. Long, Long Beard
2. Fish Juggler
3. Fisher
4. Snoozer
5. Monkey
6. Very Thirsty Fish
7. Man Slipping on Banana Peel
8. Jumping Fish
9. Dog with Bone in Mouth
10. Bone in Man's Mouth
11. Trampoline

THE RIOT AT EPHESUS
1. Flower Man
2. Statue on Skateboard
3. Giant Sub Sandwich
4. Woman with Long Hair
5. Kite
6. Mismatched Boxers
7. Snoozer
8. Big–Winded Man
9. Red Balloon
10. Basketball
11. Pink Pig

GENEROUS JERRY ENJOYS THE HOT AIR BALLOONS
1. Yo–Yo Man
2. Guitar Man
3. Whistler
4. Game of Checkers
5. Baby in Diaper
6. Yelling Sheep
7. Light Bulb
8. Hole Digger
9. Egg Juggler
10. Birdman
11. Pink Pig

JERUSALEM
1. Pumpkin
2. Cheeseburger
3. Long Beard
4. Hole in One
5. Bone in Beard
6. Welder
7. Firecracker

8. Policeman
9. Lollipop
10. Supermouse
11. Giraffe

JONAH'S LESSON
1. Mermaid
2. Clam Juggler
3. Dizzy Jellyfish
4. Six–Course Food Chain
5. Real Jellyfish
6. Snoozer
7. Smiling–Face Fish Group
8. Hammerhead Shark
9. Turtle Between Rock and Hard Place
10. Swordfish Fencing
11. Two Sea Wieners

PAUL IS SHIPWRECKED
1. Hen Balancing Six Eggs
2. Big Fish Fin
3. Fisher
4. Radio–Controlled Boat
5. Man Standing on Stool
6. Sunbather
7. Man on Swing
8. Snorkeler
9. Four Men Holding Log
10. Watermelon
11. Man Holding Two Hens

KIND CHRISTINA SPENDS A DAY AT THE ZOO
1. Boy on Pogo Stick
2. Man Reading Book
3. Sheep with Balloon
4. Whistler
5. Phone
6. Clown
7. Box of Popcorn
8. Noisy Seal
9. Shovel
10. Hungry Turtle
11. Yo–Yo Man

THE DAMASCUS ROAD
1. Roasted Marshmallow
2. Sheep Scope
3. Mama Mouse
4. Long Beard
5. Jar of Pickles
6. Guitar Man
7. Sheep in Hammock
8. Pasta Pete
9. Burger Flipper
10. Mouse in Shades
11. Bowling Ball